SCIENCE IN ACTION

The Chip

PETER JACKSON

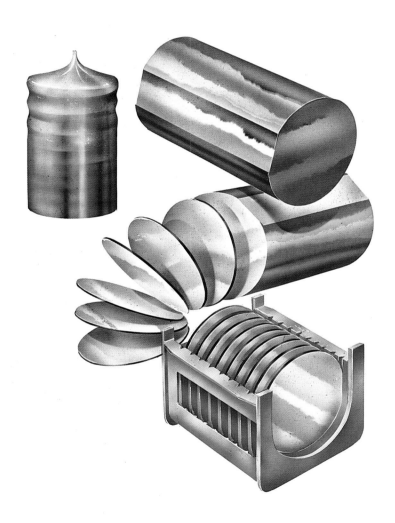

Warwick Press
New York/Toronto
1986

Published 1985 by Warwick Press,
387 Park Avenue South, New York, New York 10016.

First published in Great Britain by
Kingfisher Books Ltd.

Library of Congress Catalog Card No. 85–50829

ISBN 0–531–19006–4

Edited by Vanessa Clarke
Designed by David Jefferis
Illustrated by Mike Saunders/Jillian Burgess
Phototypeset by Waveney Typesetters, Norwich, Norfolk
Color separations by Newsele Litho Ltd, Milan, Italy
Printed in Italy by Vallardi Industrie Grafiche, Milan

Contents

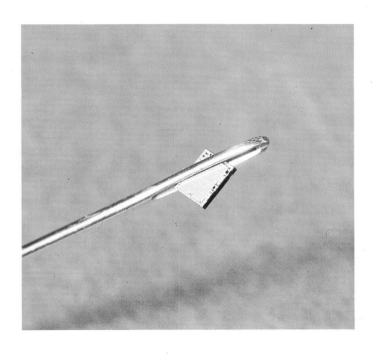

Introducing the Chip

Silicon chips are tiny things but they are causing a new kind of revolution in all our lives, as important as the Industrial Revolution which began in the 1790s. What is the chip and how can something so small be so important?

A chip is a piece of silicon less than half an inch square. It is packed with thousands of electronic circuits built in layers in the silicon itself, and sealed in a plastic case. Wires, called pins, connect the circuits with the outside world.

The Microscopic Chip

The small size of the chip makes it fast, efficient, cheap and convenient and these are the reasons why it is so important. The job that chips perform is no different from that of the printed circuit boards of electronic components which they replace. They control the flow of electricity and by doing this can be used to control hundreds of different machines or gadgets, from a toy robot to a nuclear power station.

Chips started a revolution because their minute size and low cost meant that they could be fitted into places, such as watches, where conventional circuits would take up too much space and cost too much. Because chips need little power to operate and work very fast, they were also immediately useful in batterypowered equipment and computers.

Chips at Work

Many people confuse chips with computers and think that all chips are used to make the home computers in main street stores. It is certainly true that today's computers would not exist without the chip. This is the key element that has made possible the spread of information technology – the exchange of information via computers that happens, for example, when you book a vacation, get a book from a library, pay a telephone bill or watch the weather forecast on television.

But chips also supply the controls in a whole range of products – from telephones to sewing machines, and from radios to cars. Manufacturers also use chips in the machines and robots that make these products. And this is one of the effects of the chip which worries many people: the possibility of unemployment.

It is impossible to predict exactly how the chip will affect us. But understanding what the chip is and how it works will help us to make up our minds about the kind of future we would like to see. It helps to be prepared.

◄▼ The sounds and pictures in fast-moving electronic games are produced and changed through the chips inside.

▼ With this toaster you select the type of toast you want. The chip inside then controls the heat and turns it on and off.

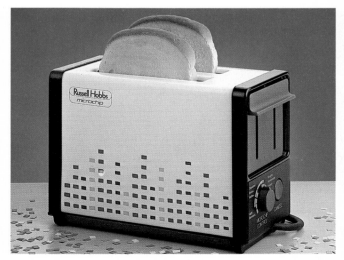

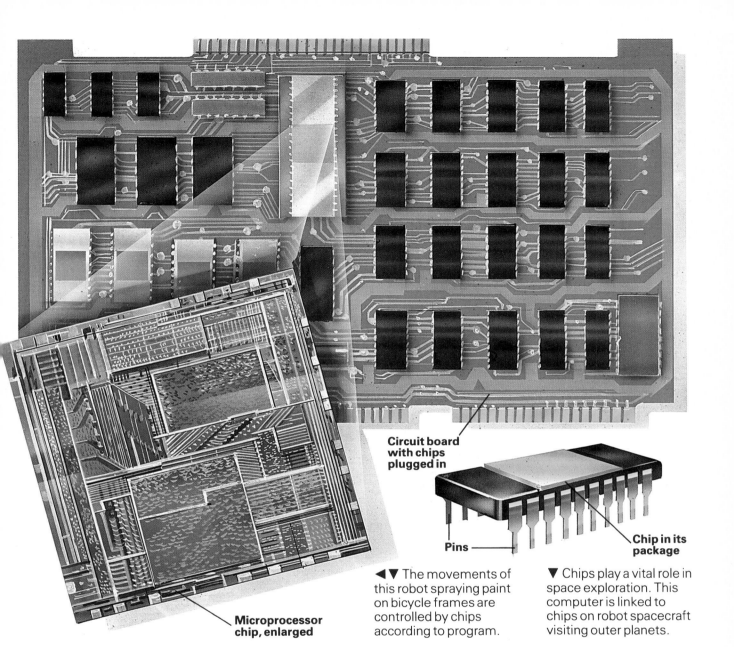

Circuit board with chips plugged in

Pins

Chip in its package

Microprocessor chip, enlarged

◄▼ The movements of this robot spraying paint on bicycle frames are controlled by chips according to program.

▼ Chips play a vital role in space exploration. This computer is linked to chips on robot spacecraft visiting outer planets.

Microelectronics

The chips in all kinds of equipment work in the same basic way. Minute currents of electricity pass along the microscopic circuits in the chip and are used to control operations of all kinds – from selecting and carrying out a washcycle in a washing machine to making high-speed calculations in a computer.

Electronics is the science of building circuits to perform operations like these, using standard electronic components. A chip is simply an electronic circuit on a very small scale – so small that chip circuitry is called microelectronics.

Transistors

The main components of the chip's circuits are transistors. These are electronic devices which can switch currents on and off or strengthen (amplify) them, depending on the conditions.

Transistors, invented in 1947, were originally made of small pieces of a semiconductor such as germanium or silicon. Scientists used semiconductors because of their physical and chemical properties. Normally, materials are of two kinds: ones that conduct electricity, such as the metals, and ones that don't, such as glass and rubber. The semiconductors are somewhere in the middle. In their pure form, as the elements silicon and germanium, they are poor conductors. But, by mixing small amounts of other elements such as boron and arsenic with the semiconductor, the properties of the material can be changed.

N-type semiconductor is made by adding arsenic, while boron produces p-type. Sandwiching lumps of p-type and n-type material together makes transistors (see opposite). Different ways of putting the p-type and n-type semiconductor together produce different types of transistors (see page 18).

The First Chip

Scientists immediately saw another possibility. Instead of sandwiching lumps of p-type and n-type together, why not produce them in a single piece of semiconductor by introducing boron and

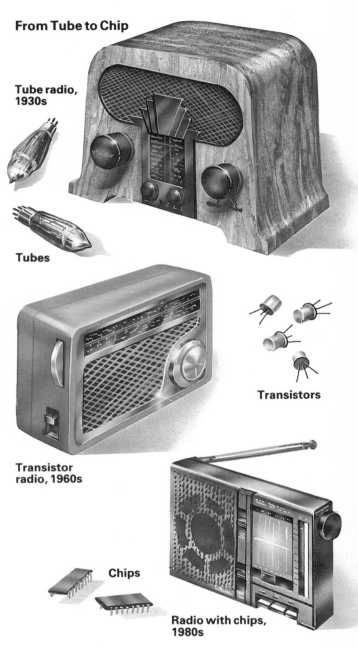

From Tube to Chip

Tube radio, 1930s

Tubes

Transistors

Transistor radio, 1960s

Chips

Radio with chips, 1980s

▲ The origin of the chip is shown here in this story of home radio sets. First came the thermionic tube. But tube radios were bulky and used lots of power. They were also unreliable as the tubes burned out like light bulbs. In 1947 the transistor replaced the tube and this led to the small battery-powered "tranny." The first silicon chips in the 1960s contained about 30 electronic components. Today a chip the same size can hold as many as 600,000 components. Radios have become smaller and do much more.

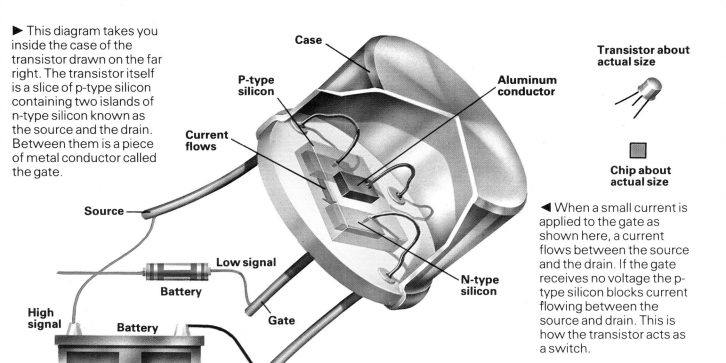

▶ This diagram takes you inside the case of the transistor drawn on the far right. The transistor itself is a slice of p-type silicon containing two islands of n-type silicon known as the source and the drain. Between them is a piece of metal conductor called the gate.

Case

P-type silicon

Current flows

Source

Low signal

Battery

High signal

Battery

Gate

Drain

Aluminum conductor

N-type silicon

Transistor about actual size

Chip about actual size

◀ When a small current is applied to the gate as shown here, a current flows between the source and the drain. If the gate receives no voltage the p-type silicon blocks current flowing between the source and drain. This is how the transistor acts as a switch.

arsenic into particular tiny areas? The result was the first integrated circuit (IC), built in 1958 in the laboratories of one of today's largest chip makers, Texas Instruments.

Here integrated means "put together in the same place." The IC consisted of a number of transistors built together and connected together on a single piece of semiconductor. It made a tiny but complete electronic circuit. The small slice of material containing the components was called a "chip" since it looked as though it had been flaked off a larger block.

There was a huge demand for the new electronic chips from the U.S. space industry. The rockets of the 1960s needed complicated electronics and needed them as small and light as possible in order to carry them into orbit.

Since then, the aim has always been to pack more and more circuits into a single piece of silicon. This has meant cheaper and cheaper electronic components, since thousands of transistors can be made simultaneously instead of one at a time. It has made the components work faster and consume less power so that circuits work more efficiently. It has also made them so small that electronics can now be built into products where it would have been impossible before.

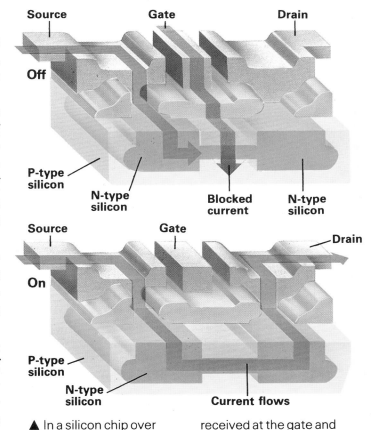

Source   **Gate**   **Drain**

Off

P-type silicon

N-type silicon

Blocked current

N-type silicon

Source   **Gate**   **Drain**

On

P-type silicon

N-type silicon

Current flows

▲ In a silicon chip over 100 transistors like the one above can be made in a space the size of this period. But they work in the same way. In the top diagram no signal is received at the gate and the current is blocked between the source and the drain. In the bottom diagram a voltage is applied to the gate and a current flows.

How Chips Work

Ordinary electronic circuits, the kind built in pre-chip days, were made up of separate components like the one shown below. The designers drew up a plan for the circuit showing where the components were to go, and how they should be connected to do the job required – to pick up and translate radio waves, for example.

Then it was just a matter of buying the components and wiring them together on a circuit board to see if they worked as planned. The designers built and tested circuits on a "breadboard", a piece of ceramic material with holes for the components and their connecting wires.

The choice of components depended on what jobs they were required to do. Diodes were used as a kind of one-way valve to let current through in one direction only around the circuit. Transistors amplified electronic signals and acted as

needed, circuit designers wire up transistors to mimic components such as resistors and capacitors. Since specially-connected transistors can also replace diodes, most silicon chips are made up entirely of transistors doing all the electronic jobs that separate components used to do.

Computers and Transistors

This is particularly true in computer chips because of their binary way of working. A computer is just a collection of switches that can be either on or off – binary "1" or "0" – connected in various ways. Everything that a computer does – receiving information, working on it, storing it or

▼ If you look inside a transistor radio, you might see a circuit board like this filled with separate components. These are linked together by copper tracks which run along the back of the circuit board.

A Radio Circuit

Coils — Capacitors — Diode — Resistors — Circuit board — Transistors — Antenna coil

▼ On this computer circuit board you can see a capacitor and several resistors wired to the chips.

switches. Resistors slowed current flow, while capacitors stored and released electric charges.

The Chip's Circuits

With the chip, the whole theory of circuit design has changed. Circuits are still made up of electronic components, but now the components are actually built in layers into the first few ten thousandths of an inch of a sliver of silicon.

Most of these components are transistors with perhaps a few diodes. Other components are difficult to make in the surface of a chip. But, if

Logic Gates

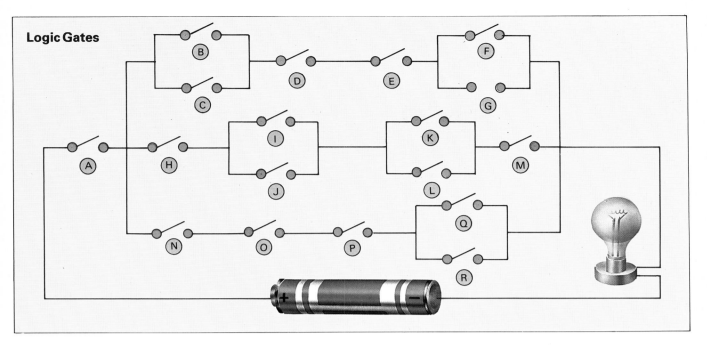

sending it out – is all done by handling strings of 1s and 0s. The strings are created by sets of transistor switches being either on or off.

Transistors make very good and very fast electronic switches. A small change of input turns the transistor completely on or off in a tiny fraction of a second (see page 11). Logic gates – the building blocks of computer circuits – and memory chips are made almost entirely of transistors.

Logic Gates

Logic gates are made simply by connecting a few transistors together and using their switching characteristics. According to certain rules of logic the gates pass on, block or change the electrical signals they receive (see above).

There are three main types of gates known as AND, OR and NOT. An AND gate has to receive two 1s before it passes on a 1. The OR gate passes on a 1 if either of the two signals it receives is a 1, and the NOT gate just reverses whichever signal it receives. Gates like these are connected together in the surface of the chip to make up complex logical circuits.

But, even in computer circuits, resistors and capacitors are needed alongside other components to set the right conditions for the transistors to work as switches. This is why you often see old-fashioned components next to chips inside computers and other chip-run equipment.

▲ Logic gates mean that something happens in a circuit only when the right conditions are met. Switch on A and (B or C) and D and E and (F or G) . . . and the lamp lights. What other routes can you take?

Binary and Decimal Numbers

128	64	32	16	8	4	2	1	
0	0	0	0	0	0	0	1	1
0	0	0	0	0	0	1	0	2
0	0	1	1	0	0	1	1	51
0	0	1	1	1	0	0	0	56
0	1	0	0	0	1	1	0	70
0	1	0	1					0
1								6
0								

Binary Codes
01000001 A
01000010 B
01000011 C
01000100 D
01000011 E
01100011 c
01100100 d
01100101 e
01000111 0 f
00011110 +
00101011 –

▲ Binary is a number code which contains only two digits, 1s and 0s. A series of 1s and 0s can represent decimal numbers. Each digit in the series is twice the value of the digit on its right. Letters and symbols can also be coded in binary. The 0s and 1s are called bits, short for *binary digits*.

Making Silicon Chips

A chip contains tens of thousands of microscopic transistors built up in layers within the surface of a silicon crystal and connected by tiny tracks of aluminum on or just below that surface. The job of the chip designer is to arrange the layout and connections of these tiny transistors to do the task required, whether the final chip is a computer memory or a sewingmachine controller. It can take years to design a complex chip like a microprocessor (see page 24), while even simple chip designs can take a team of engineers months to produce.

Computer-aided Design

Chip designers have two advantages, however. First, they have only one component to work with: the transistor. If other components are needed, such as resistors, capacitors and diodes, they connect transistors in particular ways to mimic what these components do. This is necessary in chips used as amplifiers, for instance.

Second, and more important, is that chip designers have computers to work with. Perhaps they still think up the original design in the traditional way, on the back of an envelope. But the details of which transistors go where on the final chip design are worked out on powerful computer systems.

What happens generally is that the human designer works out the layers of the chip design and enters the details into the computer using a device called a digitizer. The computer then improves it. It may point out areas of the proposed circuit that could be made more compact so that it will work faster, or suggest an alternative layout so that the circuit is easier to make.

Another method uses the computer as a design tool from the start. Computer systems can have a stock of circuit building blocks, small circuits that have been found to do a particular job well in earlier designs. If the designer finds a need in the new design for a timing circuit, for example, the computer can pull one out of store and put it on the screen in the appropriate place. In other words the computer works with the designer at

Designing a Chip

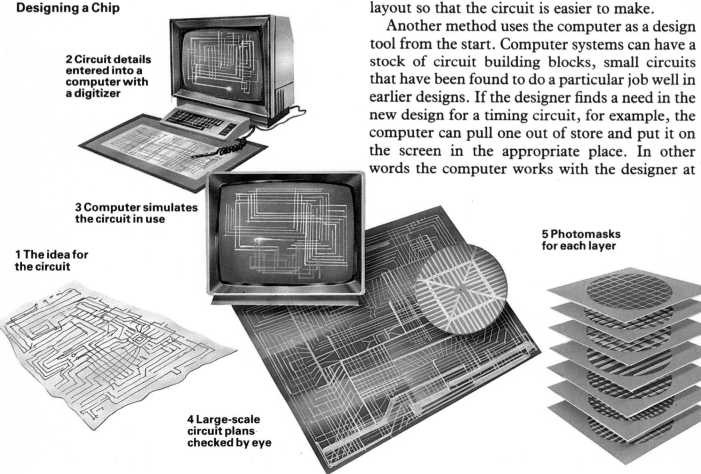

2 Circuit details entered into a computer with a digitizer

3 Computer simulates the circuit in use

1 The idea for the circuit

5 Photomasks for each layer

4 Large-scale circuit plans checked by eye

every stage – from doodling with basic ideas to tinkering with the detailed connections on the final layer of the chip.

Whether computer-aided design is used or not – and some simple chips can still be designed perfectly well by hand – the final aim is to produce a set of detailed plans, one for each layer of the chip. These are the originals for the patterns, called masks, that will be used to turn the design into chips.

Producing the Silicon

The manufacture of chips starts, naturally enough, with silicon. But although silicon is one of the commonest elements in the earth's crust, it cannot be simply taken out of the ground and made into chips. The final circuits on the chips will be so small – they are measured in ten thousandths of an inch – that any tiny defect in the silicon would interfere with the circuitry and make the chip useless.

The raw silicon must first be changed into the form of a single crystal, where all the rows of silicon atoms are lined up in an orderly manner with no holes or "ridges" of atoms. This is done by using a tiny seed crystal, a perfect single crystal, to grow a rod of exceptionally pure silicon. The rod is further purified by a method known as zone refining. Then it is sliced into thin wafers, each about 6 inches in diameter and less than a hundredth of an inch thick.

Masking

The next step is to make a set of photomasks from the designer's large-scale circuit plans. The plans are photographically reduced and duplicated so that masks containing hundreds of copies of the chip, side by side, are produced for each layer of circuits. There may be as many as a dozen. Each mask is the same size as the silicon wafer and is made of a transparent material. The circuit elements show as black.

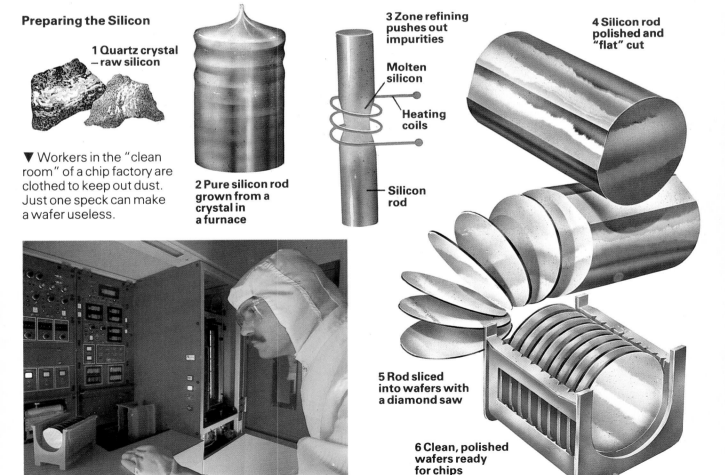

Preparing the Silicon

1 Quartz crystal – raw silicon

▼ Workers in the "clean room" of a chip factory are clothed to keep out dust. Just one speck can make a wafer useless.

2 Pure silicon rod grown from a crystal in a furnace

3 Zone refining pushes out impurities

Molten silicon

Heating coils

Silicon rod

4 Silicon rod polished and "flat" cut

5 Rod sliced into wafers with a diamond saw

6 Clean, polished wafers ready for chips

Manufacturing the Chips

The manufacture of the chips, which you can follow below, begins by growing an insulating layer of silicon dioxide across the whole surface of the wafer. This is done by exposing the wafer to oxygen in a furnace. The wafer is then coated with a light-sensitive material called photoresist and the first photomask – the one with the bottom layer of the circuit – is placed on top.

Ultraviolet light is shone on the wafer and hardens the photoresist through the transparent parts of the mask. The soft photoresist under the blacked-out parts of the mask and the silicon dioxide beneath are then washed away with acids and solvents. This opens a set of windows through the oxide to the pure silicon below.

Doping the Wafer

Tiny amounts of chemical impurities are now introduced into the wafer surface through the windows. This process is called doping. The impurities, or dopants, such as arsenic, phosphorus or boron, alter the electronic properties of the silicon and produce the n- and p-type parts of the circuits' transistors.

The most common way of introducing the dopants is to heat the wafer in a furnace, surrounded by a gaseous atmosphere of the selected impurity. A more precise method is ion implantation, where atoms of the dopant are given an electric charge and then fired into the surface of the wafer through the windows.

Once the doping for the first mask is complete, the remaining parts of the oxide layer are removed. The process is then repeated with the second mask and the appropriate impurity. Every mask is used in the same way up to the final or top layer. This mask determines the layout of the metal strips that connect the electronic components formed in the chip. This time no impurity is introduced. Instead, aluminum is laid on the surface through the windows.

Making the Chips

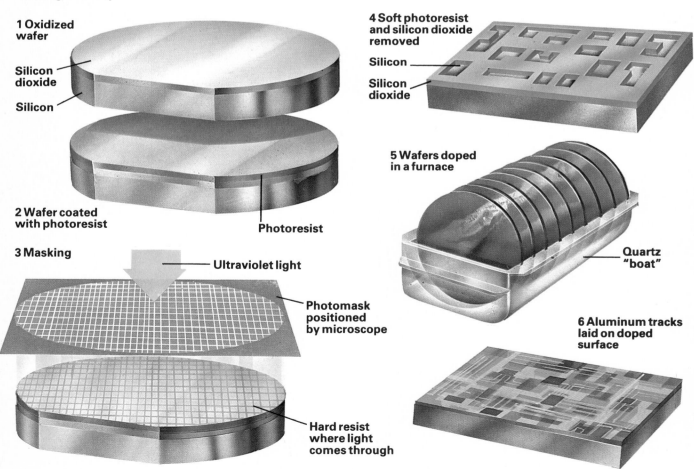

1 Oxidized wafer

Silicon dioxide

Silicon

2 Wafer coated with photoresist

Photoresist

3 Masking

Ultraviolet light

Photomask positioned by microscope

Hard resist where light comes through

4 Soft photoresist and silicon dioxide removed

Silicon

Silicon dioxide

5 Wafers doped in a furnace

Quartz "boat"

6 Aluminum tracks laid on doped surface

The correct positioning of the masks is vital because of the tiny detail involved in each chip. If a mask is out by a thousandth of an inch, the whole wafer is ruined. Powerful microscopes are used throughout the manufacturing process to check that each mask is positioned accurately.

New Techniques

Electron-beam lithography gets around the problem of mask-positioning by not using masks at all. Instead a beam of electrons is fired directly at the wafer. Where the beam hits the surface, an electron-resist hardens just as the photoresist hardens under ultraviolet light. Another method, called X-ray lithography, uses masks with a strong source of X-rays instead of ultraviolet light.

The purpose of using electrons or X-rays is simple – to get more circuitry onto each chip. Electrons and X-rays have much shorter wavelengths than ultraviolet light. This means much smaller details can be drawn and the density of components on the chip can be astronomical.

Testing the Chip

Whatever techniques are used, the final result is a wafer holding hundreds of identical chips. Each is tested with electrical probes to check that it works perfectly. Many will not because of specks of dust, operator fingerprints or any one of many possible mishaps. The percentage of chips on a wafer that works is called the yield of the chip. In the early stages of producing a new design the yield can be as low as 30 percent.

Assuming that our yield in this case is 100 per cent, the wafer is cut into individual chips with a fine diamond saw and sent for packaging. Machines weld gold wires to the chips and connect these within a frame to pins. Finally the chips are put into plastic cases and tested to make sure they work properly. They are now ready to be used in all kinds of electronic circuits.

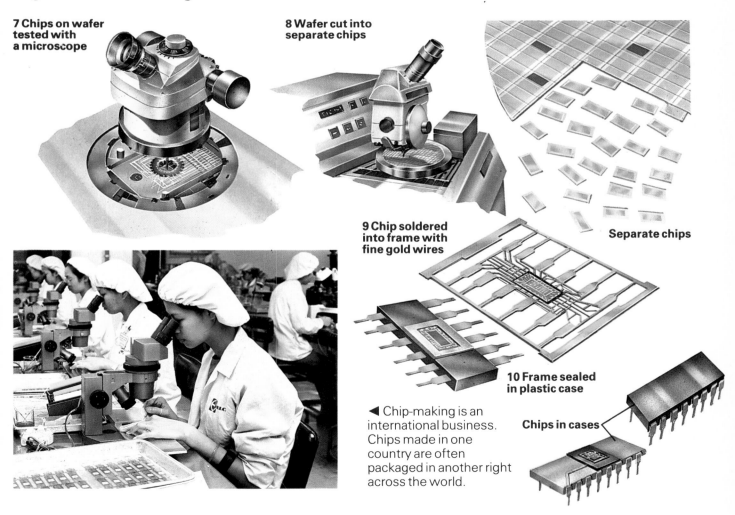

7 Chips on wafer tested with a microscope

8 Wafer cut into separate chips

Separate chips

9 Chip soldered into frame with fine gold wires

10 Frame sealed in plastic case

◀ Chip-making is an international business. Chips made in one country are often packaged in another right across the world.

Chips in cases

Chip Technology

All chips are manufactured in the same way. Tiny amounts of impurity are embedded in carefully-specified areas of a slice of silicon. Then these areas are linked with metal tracks to make electronic circuitry.

By slightly altering some parts of the process, however, different chips can be made for different types of jobs just as some cars are built for speed like the Porsche, while others are built to be economical in their use of gasoline. Chips with different characteristics are made not only by designing different circuits (see page 20) but also by building different kinds of transistors in the circuits.

Types of Transistors

The main division is between bipolar transistors and field-effect transistors. The full name of the field-effect type is metal-oxide-semiconductor field-effect transistor, MOSFET for short. Chips using MOSFETs are called MOS chips and those made up of bipolar transistors are known as bipolar chips.

Chip designers use MOS or bipolar chips according to the job that they want the chips to do. Bipolar chips work very fast and are used when speed is essential – in computers that analyze weather data, for example. CMOS, a type of MOS chip, is good for battery-powered electronic equipment such as digital watches and portable computers where low power consumption is necessary.

For most other electronic jobs, circuit designers use NMOS chips, another kind of MOS chip. The properties of NMOS provide a good average between CMOS and bipolar chips. NMOS chips also hold more circuitry than either of these types and are cheap to make.

The "metal-oxide-semiconductor" of the MOSFET name refers to the way in which the metal contacts of MOS transistors are insulated from the semiconductor surface – except where necessary for connection – by a layer of insulating oxide. Different kinds of MOS chips are made using different types of silicon to form the current channels through their transistors.

NMOS

Field-effect transistors work by narrowing or widening the current path in the transistor. It is rather like pinching a hose. When the hose is pinched tight, no water flows through the pipe. NMOS transistors have current paths of n-type silicon.

Gate open
Current flows
Hose

Gate closed

Source · Gate · Drain

Silicon dioxide

N-type silicon

P-type silicon

Bipolar

Bipolar transistors control the flow of current by raising or lowering the electrical "slope". Imagine raising a hose to cut off the flow of water inside. The structure of the bipolar transistor makes it faster than the NMOS.

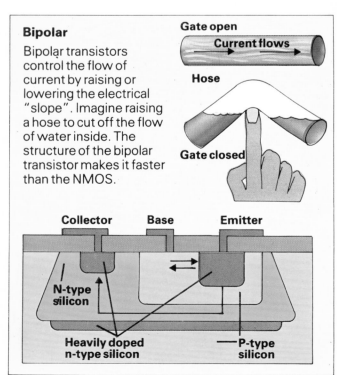

Gate open
Current flows
Hose

Gate closed

Collector · Base · Emitter

N-type silicon

Heavily doped n-type silicon

P-type silicon

Analog and Digital

Whatever transistor technology is used, there is another basic division between chips. This is the division between the digital chips used in computer and microprocessor circuits and the analog chips used in telephones, radios and all kinds of scientific equipment.

Analog circuits take smoothly varying currents and voltages as input, and produce smoothly varying currents and voltages as output. Digital circuits take in numbers, binary 1s and 0s, and produce similar numbers as output.

Both kinds of circuits are needed because the real world of sound, light and mechanical movement is an analog world where things change smoothly and not in sudden steps. But it is easier, electrically, to manipulate digital information.

▲ Military equipment must be tough and portable. The chips in this digital radio system use CMOS circuitry. They send out signals in secret codes and unscramble the messages they receive.

Analog and Digital

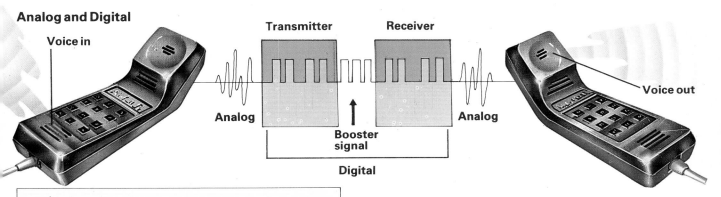

Voice in

Transmitter

Receiver

Analog

Analog

Booster signal

Digital

Voice out

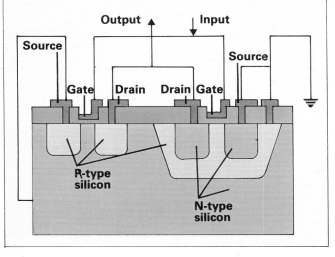

CMOS

The CMOS chip is made up of NMOS and PMOS transistors. Compare it to the NMOS chip and you will notice its extra islands of p-type material. This reduces the number of transistors that can be squeezed onto a single chip. It also makes the chip more expensive.

Output

Input

Source

Source

Gate

Drain

Drain

Gate

P-type silicon

N-type silicon

▲ Analog and digital chips are used in the telephone system. Varying voice patterns are turned into digital pulses by analog chips, transmitted as digital signals, then converted back into voices. Chips do all the conversion work.

When computers or other digital circuits are hooked up to the real world, circuits called analog-to-digital converters are used to translate the analog information into digital bits for the computer. And when the computer controls an analog process, its digital output is put through a digital-to-analog converter.

The converters bring in some inaccuracies. So, although advances are being made in digital hi-fi and television sound, for instance, most music and vision systems have lots of analog chips, called linear integrated circuits, alongside some digital ones. Both analog and digital chips can be made using MOSFETs or bipolar transistors.

Types of Chips

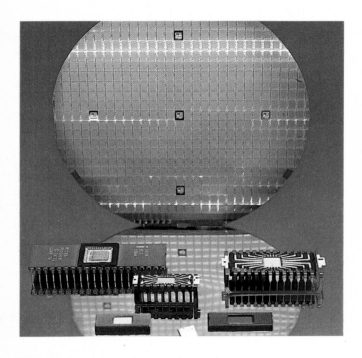

◄ The chips shown here before and after packaging are all standard chips made to carry out different tasks.

▲ The tiny chip in the viewfinder of this camera uses the ULA technique. It was the only way of making it small enough.

Whatever the technology used to make them and whether they are used in analog or digital circuits, chips are produced in three types, depending on where they will be used.

The best known type is the standard chip which is made in huge numbers, each one identical. The common microprocessors and memory circuits like those used in home computers are standard chips. Electronic circuit designers tend to use standard chips wherever possible, since the chips are mass-produced and very cheap. But a lot of effort and investment goes into making two sorts of "non-standard" chip products. In both of these the arrangement of circuits on the chip is specially chosen for a specific electronic task.

Logic arrays

The first kind of non-standard, or "custom" chip is called a logic array, an uncommitted logic array, a ULA or a gate array. All these names describe the same things – a special-purpose chip that can replace a lot of standard chips. Specially designed chips are a lot more expensive to make than standard chips, but they can make sense.

When an electronic circuit board is put together, most of the chips on it are very simple ones carrying out simple little tasks, such as adjusting voltages, inverting current signals or making sure that two particular circuits cannot operate at the same time. These little jobs can easily be done with inexpensive chips using what is called transistor-transistor logic, or TTL.

TTL chips contain only a few simple logic circuits, each with just a handful of transistors. There is no point in making them with large numbers of transistors, since then they would not be suitable for the very basic tasks they have to do. They would also cost more.

This is why many electronic circuit boards contain lots of chips. The main work is done by just a few complicated chips like microprocessors, while most of the chips – perhaps two-thirds or more – are TTL circuits doing simple electronic tasks. The idea of the logic array chip is that large numbers of TTL chips can be replaced by one single complicated chip containing many TTL circuits linked in a particular way to do a particular job. The connecting or "tailoring" is done during the final stages of manufacture.

▲ This custom chip has been specifically designed and built to fit snugly into the circuit board of a pocket calculator. Notice its square shape and the connection pads on all sides which allow the chip to lie flat.

Examples of ULAs are easy to find in home computers. Tailored logic arrays are used in some home micros to handle the screen display and communications, and in others to replace many TTL circuits. One micro has just nine chips in it, and six of those are standard memory circuits.

Custom chips

The final kind of chip is the complete custom-designed type. If standard chips are like off-the-shelf clothes, and logic arrays are like clothes that need to be altered to fit, then custom chips are tailor-made.

Since the design of a chip is very expensive, it only makes sense to design a chip for *one* special purpose if a lot of them can be made. For this reason custom chips are a lot rarer than they used to be. They are used to run digital watches and camera exposures, where the custom design is simple electronically and the cost can be spread across vast numbers of products. And they are found in military applications, where the reliability and compactness of custom chip designs is more important than cost.

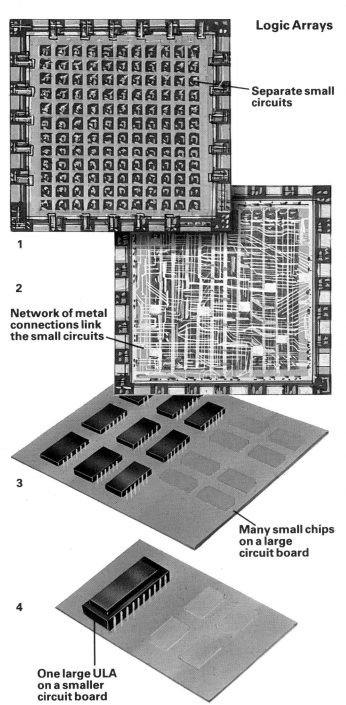

Logic Arrays

Separate small circuits

Network of metal connections link the small circuits

Many small chips on a large circuit board

One large ULA on a smaller circuit board

▲ A logic array contains hundreds of thousands of TTL logic circuits. At first none of these are connected to each other or to the chip's outside connectors (1). The designer works out a way of connecting all the logic circuits so that the logic array does the same job as lots of separate TTL chips. A final layer of tiny metal connections is then laid on top of the array chip linking the logic circuits into a particular pattern (2). In this way groups of TTL chips (3) can be replaced with one ULA chip (4). The circuit board is smaller and cheaper.

The Microprocessor Chip

When people first became aware of the chip and how it might change the way we live, it was the microprocessor that caught everyone's attention. How could a tiny piece of silicon replace a roomful of computer hardware?

The simple answer is that computers are built from electronic circuits, and any piece of electronics can be made smaller and cheaper using chips. But the microprocessor is different in one way. It packs more transistors and more complex circuitry into a smaller area than any other type of chip. As we have seen (page 12), chips carry out tasks by controlling millions of on/off currents of electricity. The more transistors a microprocessor has, the faster it can handle information and produce results.

The most powerful microprocessors process data 32 bits at a time – that is, they can manipulate binary numbers up to 32 "1"s and "0"s in length. One of the first of these, developed in 1981, contains about 250,000 transistors and produces seven watts of heat from its tiny surface.

All these transistors are necessary to do what sounds like a simple set of tasks. The microprocessor takes information from its memory or an input device, manipulates or processes this information and puts it back into the memory or to an output device. The microprocessor is told how to do each of these things by the programs stored in the memory chips (see page 24).

Inside the Microprocessor

The microprocessor chip is divided into three main areas: the arithmetic and logic unit, or ALU, the registers, and a vaguer area described as control circuits. The ALU does calculation work and manipulates the data. The registers are used as temporary storage space.

The control circuits handle the transfer of data to and from memory and the registers. They point to particular locations in memory and keep the whole chip working in time. The timing, driven by an external crystal vibrating at a very accurate frequency, is vitally important.

Buses and Pins

Connecting this internal circuitry to the circuit board and the external world are two wires divided into two main sets, called buses. These buses – called the address bus and the data bus – carry data and information from the processor to memory or input and output devices and back.

The buses run out of the microprocessor through its pins. Some of the pins connect the microprocessor to memory chips. Others are connections for the microprocessor's clock, for the power supply and for a ground connection. There may be other optional pins as well.

Instructions

Also built into each microprocessor is its instruction set. This is the collection of instructions that the processor understands and can act on. These are instructions such as "load into register zero the contents of memory location 12769", which in the microprocessor's language is just an eight-bit pattern of 1s and 0s. Each microprocessor can understand perhaps 80 different instructions of this kind, and any processing it has to do – from trigonometry to electronic ping-pong – must be made up of combinations of these instructions.

◀ This milling machine is controlled by a microprocessor.

▶ Texas Instruments 9995 microprocessor is a typical 16-bit processor.

The Microprocessor

ALU

Circuits which make all the calculations by passing signals through logic circuits that change them in various ways (see page 13).

Memory control

Includes program counter and accumulator

Accumulator

A type of register linked to the ALU. It is used when the ALU makes calculations.

Program counter

A register which always holds the address of the information or instruction that will be needed next. It keeps the program running in order.

Control circuits

Pads

Wires carrying electrical signals to the chip are welded onto the pads.

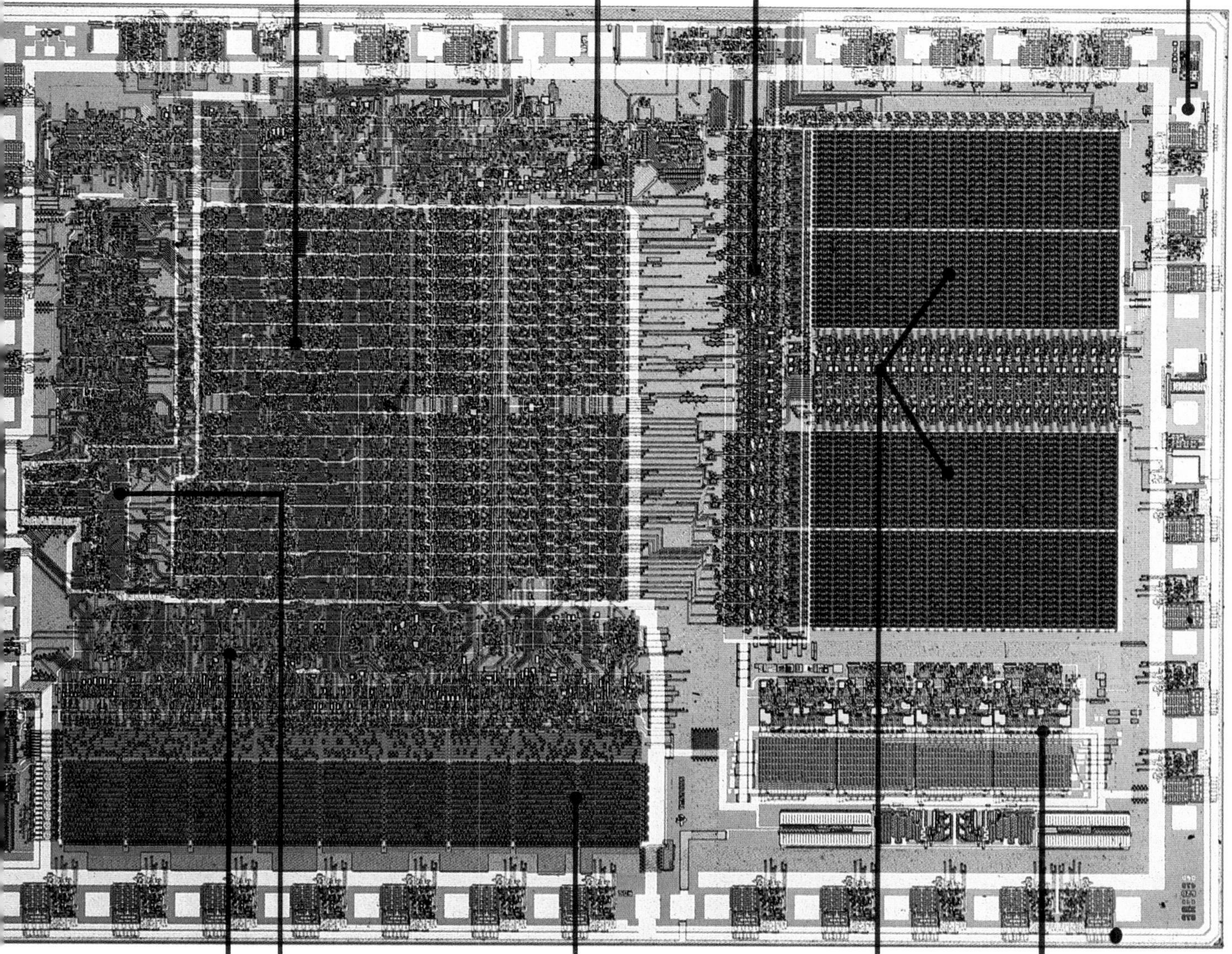

Control circuits

Instruction register

Holds the instructions which are taken by the program counter from the memory chips. It holds each one until it is replaced by the next instruction.

Instruction decoder

Part of the control circuits which holds the microprocessor's instruction set. It receives signals from the instruction register and sends out control signals to carry out the instructions.

Data registers

Registers storing information until it is needed by the ALU or results that may be needed later in the running of a program.

Clock

A group of circuits connected to a slice of quartz crystal. The regular vibrations of the crystal keep the microprocessor in time.

23

Memory Chips

Memory chips are essential parts of a microprocessor system. They store the program the processor is to run, the data needed for the program, and the results of running it.

All memory chips are designed to store information, but there are different sorts of chips for various storage jobs. The two main categories are called RAM and ROM chips.

RAM chips

Random Access Memories or RAMS are used for temporary storage. For instance they may be used to hold the program which a computer or machine is running or to store results that might be needed again later in the running of a particular program. The microprocessor can store, retrieve (fetch) and change information in RAM at any time and at great speed. But RAM chips only keep their contents as long as a power supply is provided. When the power is turned off anything stored in RAM disappears for good.

There are two kinds of RAM chip, called static and dynamic. Static RAMs are very fast, but have relatively small storage capacities. Dynamic RAMs are slower and need more complex circuitry to work, but can store huge amounts of information.

ROM chips

ROM chips, or Read Only Memories, on the other hand, hold onto their contents whether the power is off or on. These chips are always used to store programs that will be needed over and over again, such as the Basic language in a home computer or the control program in a machine.

The information on mask ROM chips is written in during the manufacturing process and can never be changed. But the contents of other types of ROM chip can be written in by the user. The PROM, or Programmable ROM, can be filled with data or programs but never changed again. Three other types – the EPROM, EAROM and EEPROM – can be filled by the user and also erased and altered later.

Bubble Memory

Bubble memory is a kind of ROM, in that it keeps its information whether the power is on or off. The information, however, is stored as a pattern of tiny magnetized regions in a chip of a semi-precious material called yttrium-aluminum-garnet. The regions, or bubbles, circulate around the chip and can be read by the processor.

Bubble memory is used less often because it is slower than the semiconductor type, more complicated to build into systems, and much more expensive. It is rugged and reliable though, and is used in battleship controls, for example, where toughness and reliability are vital.

Buses and Memory Size

All the memory chips in a microprocessor system are connected to the processor by two sets of connecting wires called buses (see below). The data

The Buses

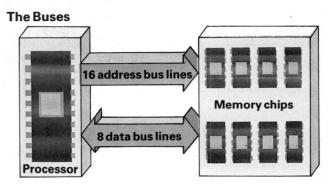

▼ The 16-bit binary number on the address bus pinpoints one particular location in the block of memory chips. The binary number there – 10011101 – is sent to the microprocessor over the eight lines of the data bus.

▲ The address and data bus connect the microprocessor to the memory chips.

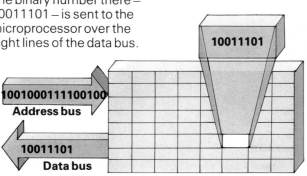

Inside a Memory Chip

This typical 64K dynamic RAM chip contains thousands of identical circuits called memory cells laid out in two blocks. The cells are arranged in columns and rows and each one holds one bit of information. Eight cells make up a memory location. Running between the blocks of memory cells are the data buses, column decoders and circuits called sense decoders.

When the microprocessor wants to store data, it sends an address code on the address bus and the data on the data bus to pads at the bottom of the chip. The address code points to particular rows and columns in the memory cells and stores the pattern of signals from the data bus.

When the microprocessor wants to fetch a piece of information, it sends the address code for the location of that information to the memory chip. A signal on the control bus tells the memory chip that the information is to be "read" out of it and the sense amplifiers put a copy of the code at that memory location onto the data bus.

Blocks of memory cells

Column decoders

Sense amplifiers

Pads where address, data and control signals enter and leave the chip

Row decoders

bus is used to transfer information to and from the processor and memory chips, and is commonly made up of eight wires to handle the contents of one memory location in one go.

The address bus is used by the processor to point to particular locations in memory (see below left). Each location has an address, a particular pattern of 1s and 0s to identify it. When the processor needs to get at a location, it puts the pattern of that location on the address bus.

Each location must have a different pattern. Therefore the size of the address bus governs the amount of memory that the processor can handle. Each wire can carry a 1 or 0, so if the address bus has 16 wires, or pins, the processor can handle up to 2^{16} – that is, 65,536 – locations; if it has 20 pins it can handle 2^{20}, or over a million locations. Because these numbers are powers of two, a special unit was invented to simplify the figures. This unit, the K, is equal to 2^{10}, that is 1,024. In these terms a 16-pin address bus gives a maximum capacity of 64K, and a 20-pin address bus gives one of 1024.

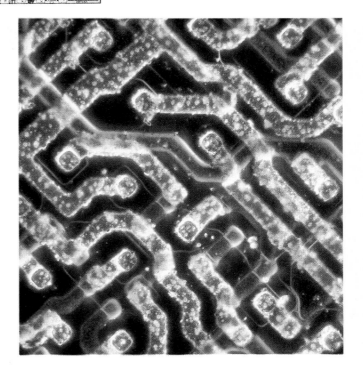

▲ A 16K memory circuit photographed at a magnification of ×160. The little squares make up memory cells and the curving lines are the metal tracks connecting the cells.

How a Microprocessor Works

Every task that a microprocessor carries out, whether it is controlling a wash-cycle in a washing machine or booking a flight in an airline computer, must be broken down into a series of instructions. These instructions make up a program, and each one must be included in the microprocessor's set.

Running a Program

One of the easiest ways to understand how a microprocessor chip carries out a job is to look at a simple program. Look at this one to add two numbers together and follow what happens in the diagram. The instructions to add the numbers, selected from the microprocessor's set, are stored in its memory chips.

At the start of the program, the microprocessor puts the address of the first instruction on the address bus wires. The contents of the memory location at this address are, in response, put onto the data bus wires and read into the instruction register inside the microprocessor. Our simple program has an instruction saying "load the accumulator register with the number 2." Like the instruction, the number "2" is coded into a pattern of eight 1s and 0s, a unit called a byte. The processor recognizes the instruction byte and loads the accumulator register with the binary number representing the decimal number "2."

While this is happening the program counter has automatically increased by one and now holds the address of the next instruction in the program. This in turn goes onto the address bus, and the contents of this location are sent to the processor on the data bus and the instruction decoded. In our program, this is another pattern of binary digits meaning "load register zero with the number 2." The microprocessor puts the binary version of "2" into another of its registers.

The next instruction the processor finds is "add to the accumulator the contents of register zero." The ALU section of the chip uses its logic gates to add the binary "2" in register zero to the binary "2" in the accumulator, and leave the result there.

Finally we need to store the answer in memory for future reference. So the last instruction the microprocessor receives is "store the contents of the accumulator in memory location x." Here x is an empty location in memory. The processor then puts the address x on its address bus, and the contents of the accumulator go over the data bus into that location.

Electronic Speed

As you can see, all this little program has done is add two and two, which any of us can do in our heads. But the difference is that the microprocessor can do this simple calculation about a million times in one second.

It takes hundreds of thousands of instructions like these from its instruction set for a microprocessor to book you an airline ticket to Paris or complete a washing cycle. But the microprocessor does not get tired or make a mistake. Its power is not in its cleverness but in the speed of its electronic circuits and the circuits of the memory and interface chips that support it.

▼ A simple 2+2 adding program. It breaks the task into a series of small steps.

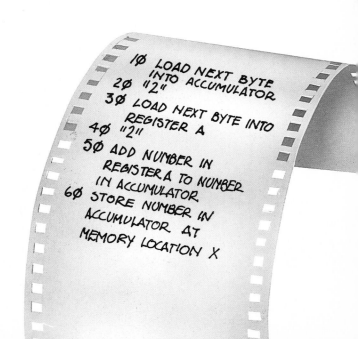

10 LOAD NEXT BYTE INTO ACCUMULATOR
20 "2"
30 LOAD NEXT BYTE INTO REGISTER A
40 "2"
50 ADD NUMBER IN REGISTER A TO NUMBER IN ACCUMULATOR
60 STORE NUMBER IN ACCUMULATOR AT MEMORY LOCATION X

▲ The microprocessor (center above) controls the motor, heater and instrument panel of this washing machine. It receives information from sensors and uses it to carry out selected washing programs.

▼ The diagram shows how a microprocessor carries out the program. Each byte of the program is collected from the memory chip at the bottom and passed one by one through the processor's circuits.

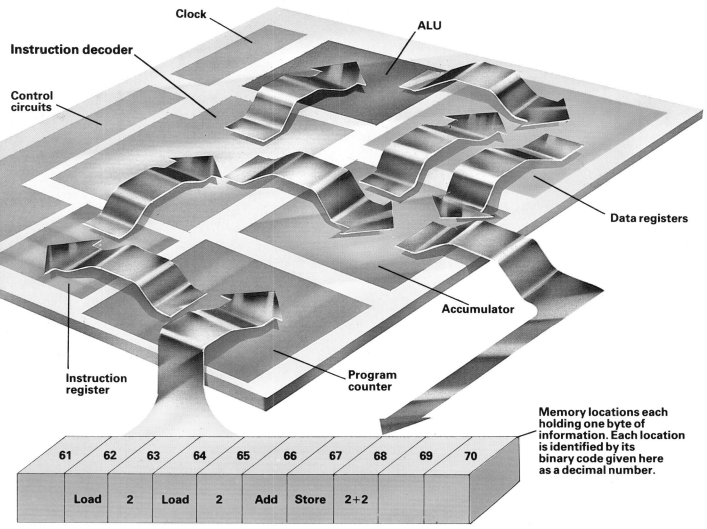

Clock

ALU

Instruction decoder

Control circuits

Data registers

Accumulator

Instruction register

Program counter

Memory locations each holding one byte of information. Each location is identified by its binary code given here as a decimal number.

61	62	63	64	65	66	67	68	69	70
	Load	2	Load	2	Add	Store	2+2		

Chips and the Computer

The computers of today would not be possible without the chip. Some form of computer would exist using separate transistors connected with wire, but they would look nothing like the home and business computers we know and would not perform nearly as well.

A computer is not just a microprocessor. In fact some computers do not use microprocessors at all except for backup tasks such as entering data. The largest and fastest and most powerful computers in the world, like those used to analyze geological data in the search for oil or to relate the vast masses of weather data collected from around the world, need more speed than the standard microprocessor can produce.

Supercomputers

As we have seen, bipolar chips (page 18) are faster than MOS chips such as the typical microprocessor. Bipolar chips in which the transistors are connected using a method called emitter-coupled logic are particularly fast and these are the processor chips found in really big computers, in larger business mainframes and in scientific minicomputers. These processors do the same job in the system as the microprocessor does in a home computer. But they do it very much faster, with more accuracy and with access to more data and memory space at once.

The Home Computer System

Most of the computers that we come across in everyday life – in schools, the home and small businesses – are built around a standard microprocessor chip connected to standard memory chips. The number and size of the memory chips depend on the amount of memory the microprocessor can handle (see page 25) and on the computer's design.

Apart from the microprocessor and memory chips, the most important chips in a typical computer system are the chips that link the processor with input and output devices. These input and output chips, often called interface

▲ The CRAY-1 is the fastest and most powerful computer in the world. The processor is contained in these cylindrical structures.

▼ Computers are essential tools for making complex chips. Here a chip designer is laying out a circuit using a digitizer and a keyboard.

chips, code electrical signals from the outside world into the binary 1s and 0s that the microprocessor and memory chips understand. They also translate the code back into the electrical signals that output equipment uses.

Parallel and Serial

Computers communicate with the outside world in two main ways, with parallel or serial data. Parallel means that information is sent out on a set

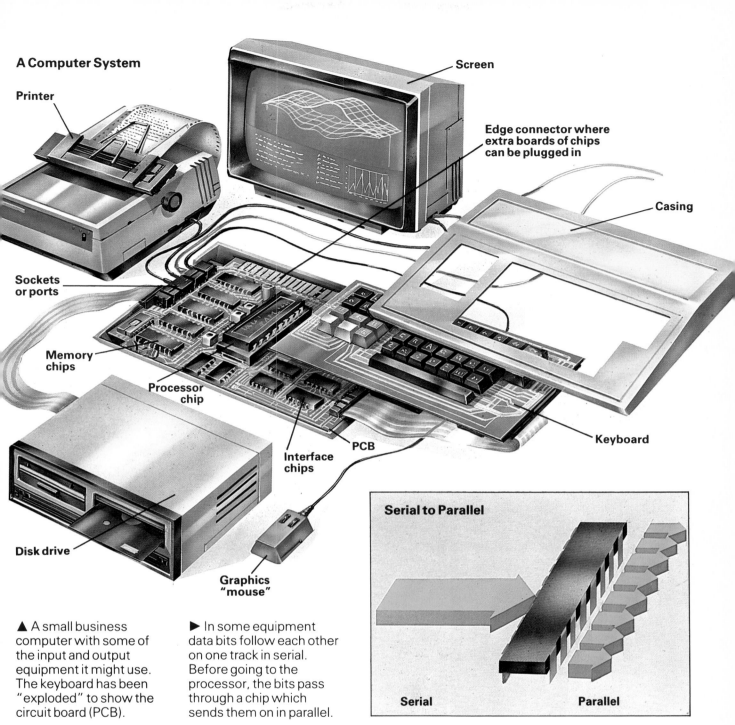

A Computer System

Printer

Screen

Edge connector where extra boards of chips can be plugged in

Casing

Sockets or ports

Memory chips

Processor chip

Interface chips

PCB

Keyboard

Disk drive

Graphics "mouse"

Serial to Parallel

Serial

Parallel

▲ A small business computer with some of the input and output equipment it might use. The keyboard has been "exploded" to show the circuit board (PCB).

▶ In some equipment data bits follow each other on one track in serial. Before going to the processor, the bits pass through a chip which sends them on in parallel.

of wires, a number of binary digits at a time. Serial means that the information is sent out along one wire, one bit at a time. Chips called things like PIO (parallel input/output) and SIO (serial input/output) devices handle these functions.

Other Chips

The microprocessor, memory and input/output chips are necessary for any computer to work. The other chips that might be found in a computer like the one above depend on the design of the computer and where it is used. A computer in a bank, for example, might have a network controller chip to let it connect up with other computers. An industrial computer is almost certain to have analog-to-digital and digital-to-analog chips to gather information from and control analog machinery. Whatever chips a computer uses, they are all there to help the computer work efficiently.

Chips and Industry

Chips are not just making an impact in the computer world. They are also revolutionizing the way things are made in manufacturing industries and the design of all sorts of products.

Chips in Industry

Chips are having a dramatic effect in manufacturing because they can be used for such a wide range of tasks – from controlling a metal-cutting tool to visually checking a conveyor belt loaded with cakes and picking out the squashed ones. The most common way of using chips is to build computer power into the machines that the factory uses and to use computerized monitoring systems to control the process of manufacture from start to finish.

As usual, putting chips into things makes them smaller, cheaper and more efficient. Using chips to drive machines and monitor processes means more accurate control, less wastage and, in hazardous processes such as steel manufacture, less danger to the workforce.

The computer power can either be added to existing machinery or a new style of machine can be built around the chip. This kind of machine is the industrial robot.

Robots

The robot is just a computer-controlled machine built to do one job or many different jobs. It might spray paint on car bodies, push the knob that moves the hands into watches or check that the label is the right side up on bottles of tomato ketchup. The one certain thing is that it is controlled by the chip and carries out its task or tasks according to programs.

Robots and computer-controlled machines on the factory floor need fewer humans to control and supervise them. But there must be some human intelligence deciding what they are programmed to do. Even these humans, however, get assistance from chips built into computers that help to design products, organize the manufacturing process and handle sales.

Products with Chips

Count the number of electric motors in your home: you'll probably be surprised at how many there are – in things such as hairdryers, refrigerators, and heating systems. And chips are moving into the home, often alongside those motors.

Two of the first products to use chips were digital watches and electronic calculators. The first models of these were expensive because they were made in small numbers. The chips were crude too, and only a few in each batch worked. But very quickly the chips improved; the numbers made went up and the price came down. Now the price stays the same but the functions of a watch or calculator increase all the time.

A similar process is happening with other equipment. Chips are making all sorts of products cheaper by cutting down on moving parts. At the same time they are making products more attractive by offering the user more functions at the same price.

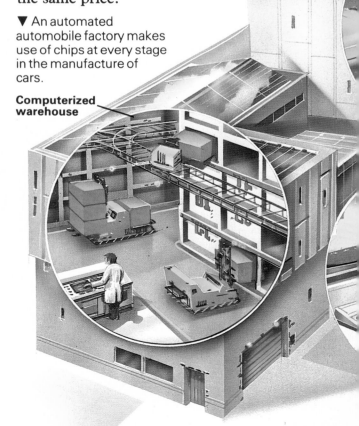

▼ An automated automobile factory makes use of chips at every stage in the manufacture of cars.

Computerized warehouse

Custom and Standard Chips

Most of the chips used in big home appliances such as ovens are custom chips (see page 20). They are single chips with circuits designed to do specific jobs according to programs selected by the user at a touch of a button. These chips are also specially designed to withstand extremes of temperature, pressure and vibration, just like the chips made for use in tanks and missiles. Other products, such as toys, toasters and cameras, use standard or semi-custom chips.

In science fiction, the home of the future is often controlled by one friendly computer that does everything from turning on the lights and making coffee to saving energy in the central heating system. Instead, chips that do one job instead of many are being used. It may not be spectacular but the chip-driven home is already here in the products we use.

▲ A portable hi-fi system provides the music for this street entertainer. Inside it are circuits containing both analog and digital chips.

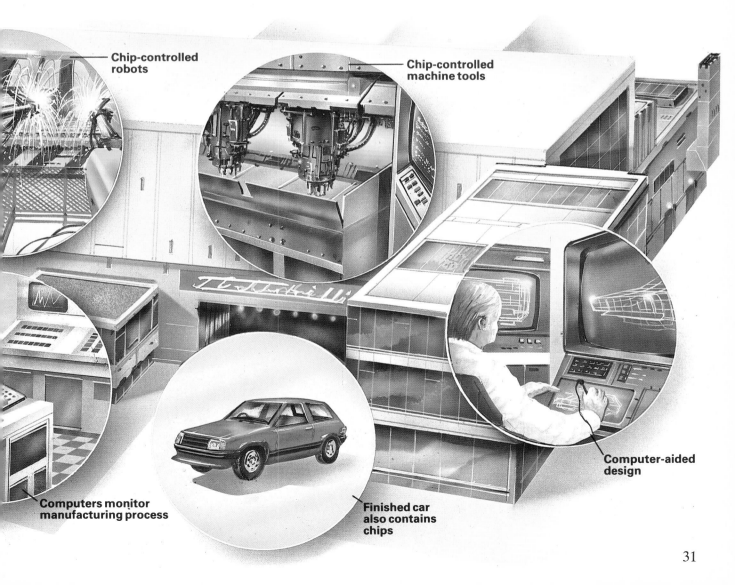

Chip-controlled robots

Chip-controlled machine tools

Computer-aided design

Computers monitor manufacturing process

Finished car also contains chips

The Future

The silicon revolution has happened so quickly that it is sometimes hard to step back and think about its future. But developments are already under way to take the chip into its next phase.

The most fundamental change could be in the material that the chips are made of. Chip designers are experimenting with two man-made materials, gallium arsenide (GaAs) and indium antimonide.

Silicon has lots of life left, however. The main research here is on producing more and more complicated chips. Today's chips include components smaller than ten-thousandth of an inch across and contain around 250,000 transistors. For the future researchers are talking about cramming millions of transistors on a single chip. Even with advanced production techniques, this means making larger chips.

Wafer Chips
So why not go all the way and use the whole area of the wafer for one chip? The number of transistors could then be millions. But most companies investigating this possibility have found the technical problems too great.

These problems are mainly to do with the material used – the silicon itself. Even the purest silicon crystals made have some defects. The atomic layout of the crystal may have a hole or a slipped layer of atoms.

Wafer-size chips need super-pure silicon crystals and they are very hard to make – at least on earth. Many of the defects in the crystal are caused by the pull of gravity while the crystals are growing. Only in "free fall" conditions, such as in orbit around the earth, where gravity does not exist, can these defects be avoided.

Space Silicon
Astronauts in the U.S. Space Shuttle have carried out experiments in growing silicon crystals. In the future, space industries could produce a whole new generation of big chips just by making purer silicon available in quantity.

The low temperatures of space, brought down to earth, could lead to another new kind of chip – the superconductor. At these low temperatures, not far above Absolute Zero, $-273°$ Celsius, scientists have discovered that certain materials become superconductors. This means that once a current flow has been started in the material, it will continue indefinitely without losing energy.

Josephson Junctions
Experimental circuits using superconductivity have been built by IBM. They are called Josephson junctions after their inventor, a Cambridge physicist. Only simple logic circuits have been produced, but their processing speed is remarkable. It has to be measured in nanoseconds and picoseconds, where a nanosecond is one billionth of a second and a picosecond is one thousand times shorter than that.

▼ A technician lowers a Josephson junction into a container of liquid helium at an IBM research lab.

▶ An artist's impression of a free-fall chip factory in space. Superpure silicon may lead to the wafer chip.

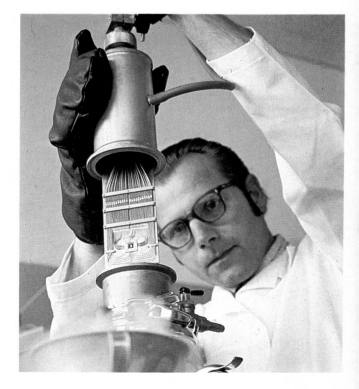

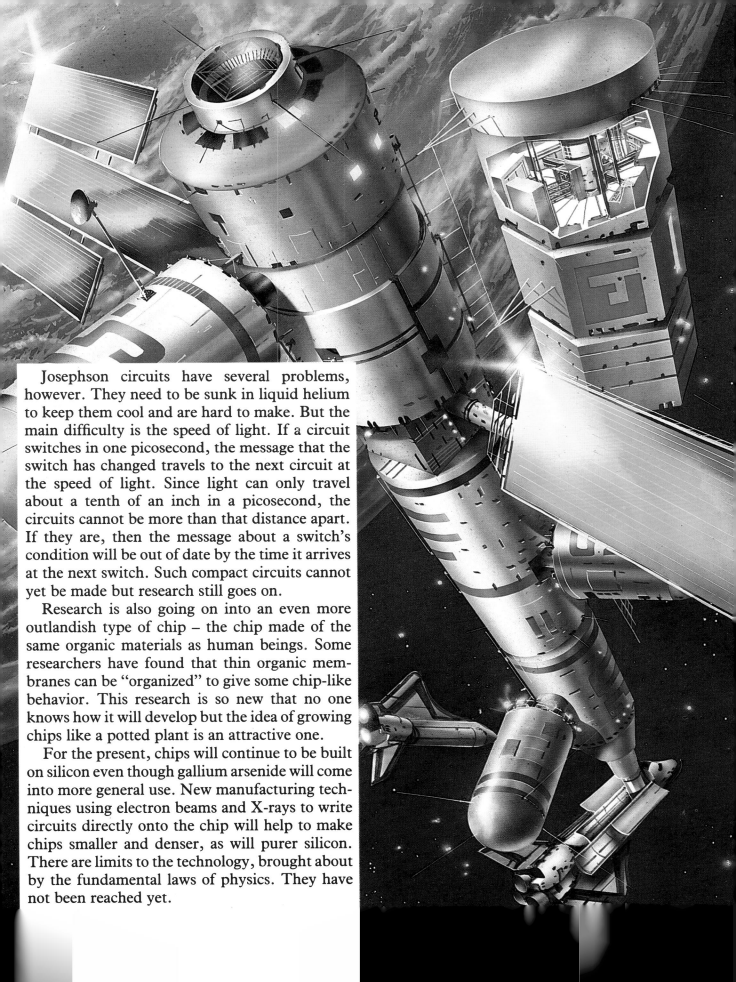

Josephson circuits have several problems, however. They need to be sunk in liquid helium to keep them cool and are hard to make. But the main difficulty is the speed of light. If a circuit switches in one picosecond, the message that the switch has changed travels to the next circuit at the speed of light. Since light can only travel about a tenth of an inch in a picosecond, the circuits cannot be more than that distance apart. If they are, then the message about a switch's condition will be out of date by the time it arrives at the next switch. Such compact circuits cannot yet be made but research still goes on.

Research is also going on into an even more outlandish type of chip – the chip made of the same organic materials as human beings. Some researchers have found that thin organic membranes can be "organized" to give some chip-like behavior. This research is so new that no one knows how it will develop but the idea of growing chips like a potted plant is an attractive one.

For the present, chips will continue to be built on silicon even though gallium arsenide will come into more general use. New manufacturing techniques using electron beams and X-rays to write circuits directly onto the chip will help to make chips smaller and denser, as will purer silicon. There are limits to the technology, brought about by the fundamental laws of physics. They have not been reached yet.

Glossary

Address An address is a number that specifies a particular location in a memory chip; each location has a unique address. See **bus**.

Analog Analog circuits, as opposed to **digital** circuits, work with smoothly-varying quantities; also called linear integrated circuits.

Bipolar Bipolar chips are built using the bipolar type of **transistor**, and are faster but less dense than **MOS** types.

Bubble memory A type of memory chip that is slower and more expensive than **semiconductor** memory chips, but does keep its contents when power is removed and is very rugged.

Bus A set of parallel wires designed to connect chips with each other; the address and data buses of a **microprocessor** are examples.

CAD Stands for computer-aided design, much used in working out the designs of new chips.

Chip A tiny piece of silicon with a microelectronic circuit built into its surface.

CMOS A way of building **NMOS** and **PMOS** transistors into a chip to produce circuits with very low power consumption. CMOS stands for *c*omplementary *m*etal-*o*xide-semiconductor.

Custom chips Chips specially designed from scratch for a particular job.

Digital The opposite of **analog**; digital chips work with numerical quantities only.

Digitizer A drawing board connected to a **CAD** system, used to transfer design drawings from paper to the computer.

DIP Stands for *d*ual *i*n-line *p*ackage; the beetle-like chips on a typical circuit board are protected in DIP cases.

Doping Introducing various impurities (dopants) into particular areas of a chip or wafer to create the electronic circuit.

Dynamic A form of **RAM** chip that needs special circuitry around it to work, but has great storage density. The special circuits must be constantly "refreshed" in order to keep their charges.

Electron beam lithography A method of drawing circuit elements directly onto the surface of a chip, without using a **mask.**

Field-effect transistor A type of transistor using the squeezing of a current channel to control its operation; comes in n-channel and p-channel types.

Gallium Arsenide A man-made semiconductor made by mixing the elements gallium and arsenic; gallium arsenide chips are faster than **silicon** ones, but harder to make.

Gate array A type of chip where all the components are the same, but unconnected; a top layer of metal connections determines what the chip will do. See **ULA.**

Germanium A semiconductor material similar in properties to **silicon**, but slightly inferior for chip production.

Integrated circuit A number of electronic components such as transistors, built and connected together in a single **semiconductor** chip.

Ion implantation A way of putting impurities into a chip to make the circuits; the atoms of the impurity are charged and fired into the chip by magnetic fields.

Josephson junction A futuristic type of chip that works in a bath of liquid helium and uses **superconductivity**; it can switch billions of times per second.

Mask A layer of a chip design; a pattern placed on top of a chip to outline where the impurities are to go to make up the circuits.

Microprocessor A complex chip that processes digital information; the heart of microcomputers.

MOS Stands for *metal oxide semiconductor*, and describes a way of building transistors with layers of metal and silicon dioxide on top of silicon.

Nanosecond A length of time equal to one billionth of a second (1 billion $= 10^9$).

NMOS The most common sort of chip; a design using n-channel **MOS field-effect transistors.**

PCB Stands for *printed-circuit board*; a ceramic board with metal tracks engraved on it, on which the chip **DIP**s are soldered to make circuits.

Photolithography A way of outlining the circuits on a chip by shining ultraviolet light through a design **mask** to harden **photoresist** in specific areas.

Photoresist A material that hardens on exposure to ultraviolet light; used in **photolithography** to mark out areas where the doping impurities go.

Picosecond A length of time equal to a thousand-billionth of a second (10^{-12} seconds).

PMOS A chip design using p-channel **MOS fiield-effect transistors.**

RAM Stands for *random access memory*; a type of memory chip used for temporary storage, which loses its contents when the power supply is removed.

Register A temporary storage location inside a **microprocessor** chip, used to store the data it is manipulating.

ROM Stands for *read only memory*; a type of memory chip that keeps its contents permanently, used to store permanent programs.

Semiconductor A material that is neither a good insulator nor a good conductor of electricity. Its electrical properties can be altered by adding impurities.

Silicon A particular semiconductor material used in the majority of all chips; one of the most common elements in the earth's crust.

Static The opposite of **dynamic**; a type of **RAM** chip that needs no external circuitry to work, but can store less information per chip.

Superconductivity A property of certain metals, which lose all electrical resistance at temperatures near the absolute zero of $-273°C$.

Transistor An electronic component that can be used as a switch or an amplifier; the principal component of microelectronic circuits.

TTL Stands for *transistor-transistor logic*; a way of connecting transistors together to perform logical operations, much used on computer boards.

Tube Short for thermionic tube; an outdated electronic component using a hot filament and metal grids in a vacuum to switch and amplify voltage and current.

ULA Stands for *uncommitted logic array*; like a gate array, this is a semi-**custom** chip that can be tailored to do a particular job by adding a top layer of metal connections.

Wafer A slice of silicon about 6 inches across, on which perhaps a thousand chips are made simultaneously.

X-ray lithography A method of drawing circuits on a chip through a **mask**; the short wavelength of X-rays means that smaller details can be drawn than with **photolithography.**

Zone refining A method of purifying a single crystal of silicon by passing a moving band of heating along the crystal rod; the impurities are caught up by the moving molten band.

Index

Note: Page numbers in *italics* refer to illustrations.

ACKNOWLEDGEMENTS

Front cover: bottom left: Zilog Inc, middle: Cray Research Inc, bottom right: Hong Kong Tourist Board; 7: STC Components Ltd; 8 left: Martin Dohrn/SPL, right: Russell Hobbs Ltd; 9 left: Trallfa Nils Underhang A/S, right: Jet Propulsion Laboratory; 12: Grapes/Michaud/SPL; 15: Zilog Inc; 17: Hong Kong Tourist Board; 19: Marconi Secure Radio Systems Inc; 20 left: Siltec Corp, right: Ferranti PLC; 21: Martin Dohrn/SPL; 22: Austin Rover Group Ltd; 23: Texas Instruments; 25 top: STC Components Ltd, bottom right: S. Stammers/SPL; 27: Hoover PLC; 28 top: Cray Research Inc, middle: Plessey Semiconductors Ltd; 31: Steve Beer; 32: IBM.

Picture research: Penny J. Warn.